The Adventures of Pookie Presents:

My Family Tree

Rebecca Yee

This book is for you to be creative. Paste pictures, use stickers, color in it, write in it, and keep track of your family tree!

Family is one of the most important things in the world. Have your parents help you do some research and learn as much as you can.

Use the memories pages to add photos of your family, your pets, your grandparents, and anything that is important to you.

Use the extra notes pages to write down anything that you learn about your family and their history.

About Me

My Name

your picture
here

_____

First   Middle   Last

MyBirthdate

_____

Month   Day   Year

I was born in...

_____

City, State, Country

♥ My ♥ Brothers/Sisters	🐾 My Pets 🐾	🧩 My Cousins 🧩

About Dad

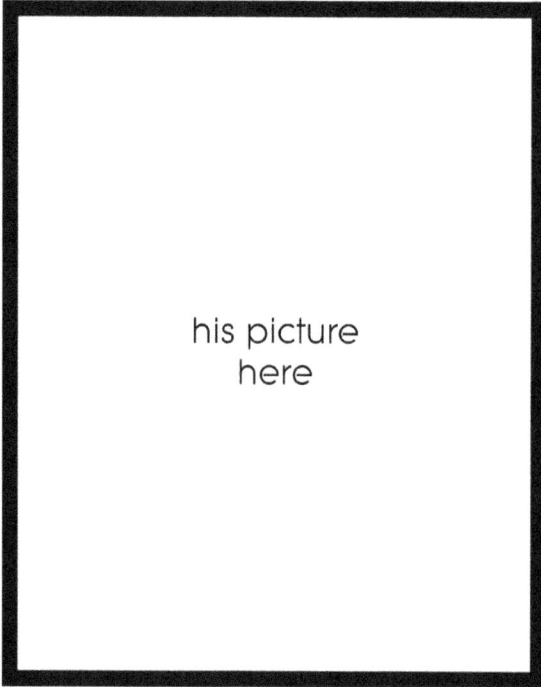

his picture here

His Name

_____

First   Middle   Last

His Birthdate

_____

Month   Day   Year

He was born in...

_____

City, State, Country

♥ His Brothers/Sisters ♥
(My Aunts/Uncles)

His Cousins

About Mom

Her Name

_____

First   Middle   Last (Maiden)

Her Birthdate

_____

Month   Day   Year

her picture
here

She was born in...

_____

City, State, Country

♥ Her Brothers/Sisters ♥
(My Aunts/Uncles)

Her Cousins

About Grandpa

My Dad's Dad

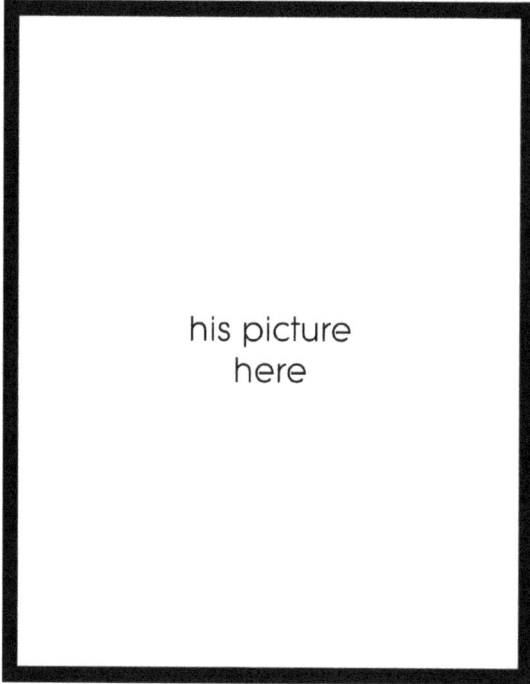

his picture here

His Name

_____

First   Middle   Last

His Birthdate

_____

Month   Day   Year

He was born in...

_____

City, State, Country

♥ His Brothers/Sisters ♥

His Cousins

About Grandma

My Dad's Mom

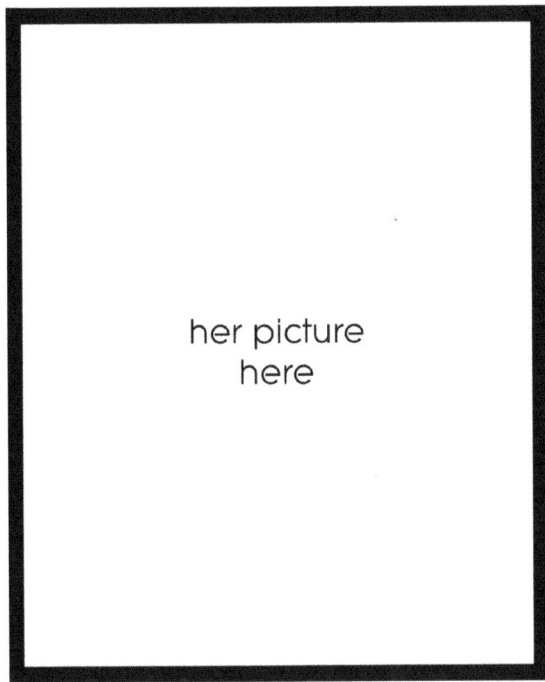

her picture
here

Her Name

_____

First   Middle   Last (Maiden)

Her Birthdate

_____

Month   Day   Year

She was born in...

_____

City, State, Country

♥ Her Brothers/Sisters ♥

Her Cousins

About Grandpa

My Mom's Dad

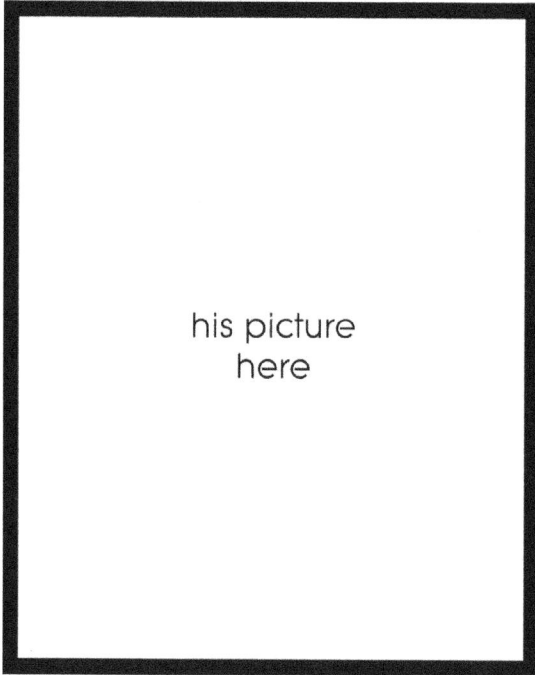

his picture
here

His Name

_____

First   Middle   Last

His Birthdate

_____

Month   Day   Year

He was born in...

_____

City, State, Country

♥ His Brothers/Sisters ♥	His Cousins

About Grandma

My Mom's Mom

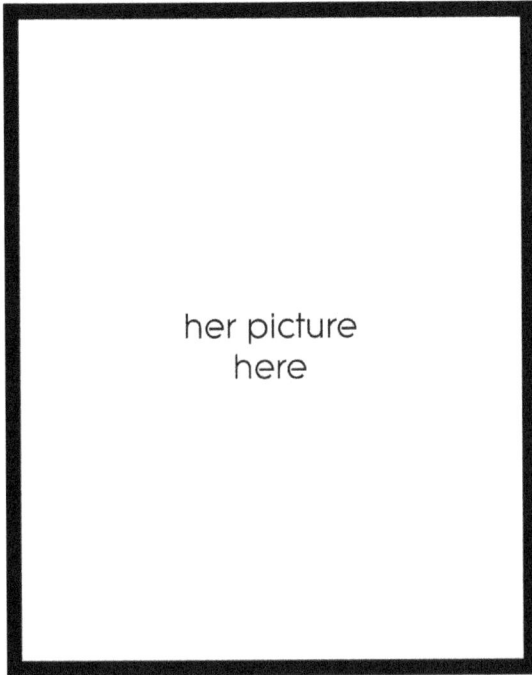

her picture
here

Her Name

_____

First   Middle   Last (Maiden)

Her Birthdate

_____

Month   Day   Year

She was born in...

_____

City, State, Country

♥ Her Brothers/Sisters ♥

Her Cousins

About Great Grandpa

My Dad's Grandpa

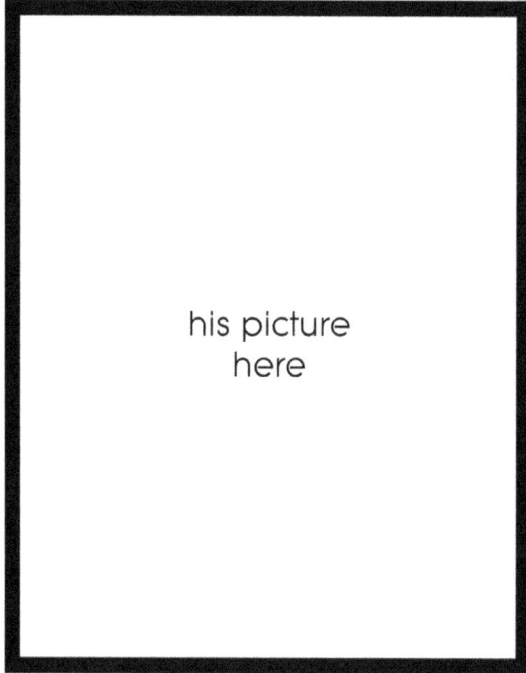

his picture
here

His Name

_____

First   Middle   Last

His Birthdate

_____

Month   Day   Year

He was born in...

_____

City, State, Country

♥ His Brothers/Sisters ♥

🧩 His Cousins 🧩

About Great Grandma

My Dad's Grandma

her picture
here

Her Name

_____

First   Middle   Last (Maiden)

Her Birthdate

_____

Month   Day   Year

She was born in...

_____

City, State, Country

♥ Her Brothers/Sisters ♥

Her Cousins

About Great Grandpa

My Mom's Grandpa

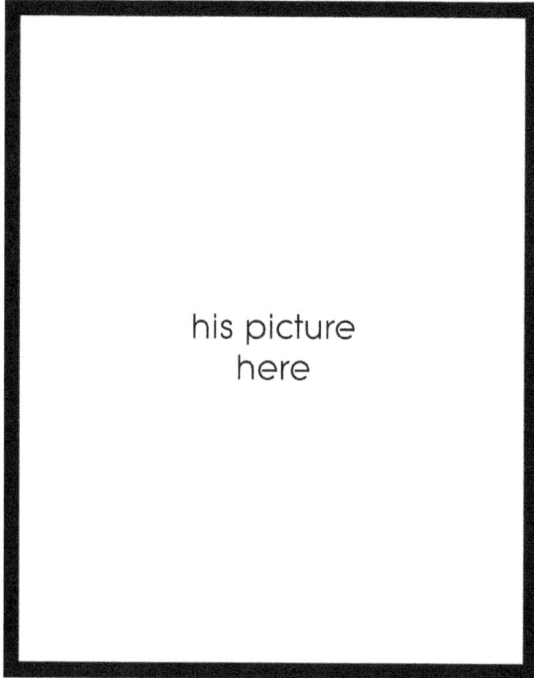

his picture
here

His Name

_____

First   Middle   Last

His Birthdate

_____

Month   Day   Year

He was born in...

_____

City, State, Country

♥ His Brothers/Sisters ♥

His Cousins

About Great Grandma

My Mom's Grandma

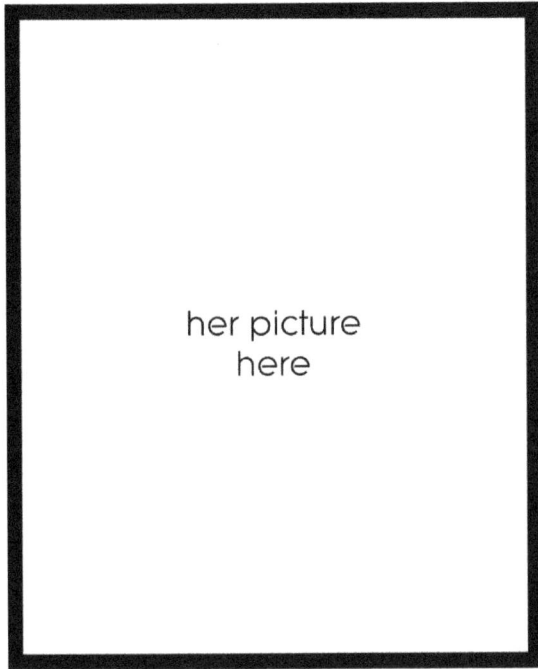

her picture
here

Her Name

_____

First   Middle   Last (Maiden)

Her Birthdate

_____

Month   Day   Year

She was born in...

_____

City, State, Country

♥ Her Brothers/Sisters ♥

Her Cousins

About Great-Great Grandpa

My Dad's Great Grandpa

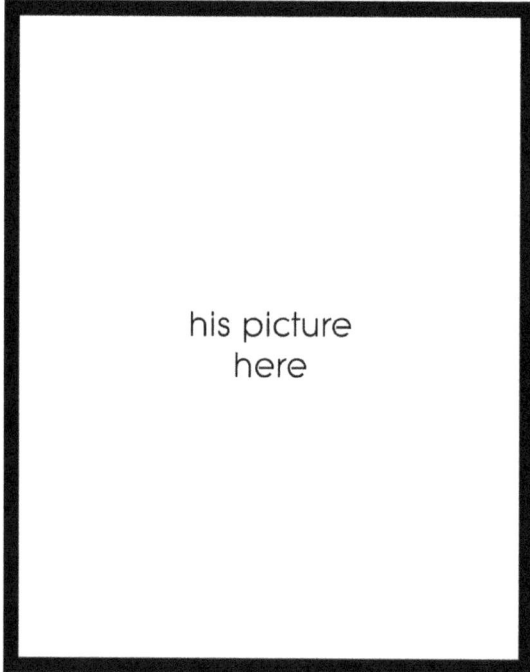

his picture
here

His Name

_____

First   Middle   Last

His Birthdate

_____

Month   Day   Year

He was born in...

_____

City, State, Country

♥ His Brothers/Sisters ♥

His Cousins

About Great-Great Grandma

My Dad's Great Grandma

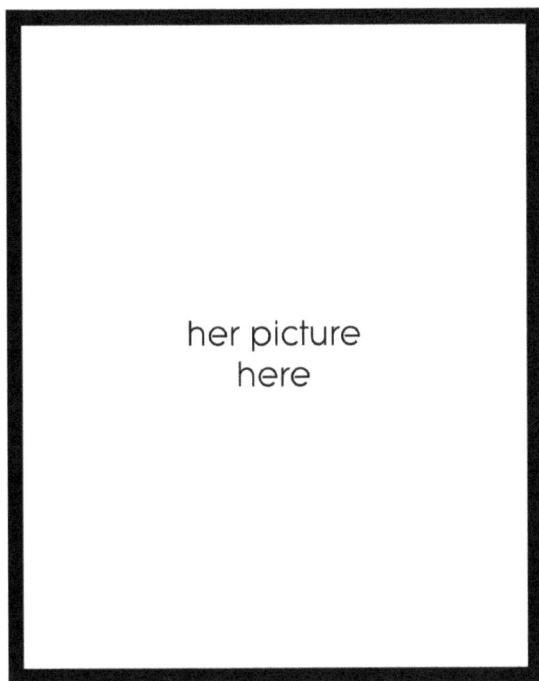

her picture
here

Her Name

_____

First   Middle   Last (Maiden)

Her Birthdate

_____

Month   Day   Year

She was born in...

_____

City, State, Country

♥ Her Brothers/Sisters ♥

🧩 Her Cousins 🧩

About Great-Great Grandpa

My Mom's Great Grandpa

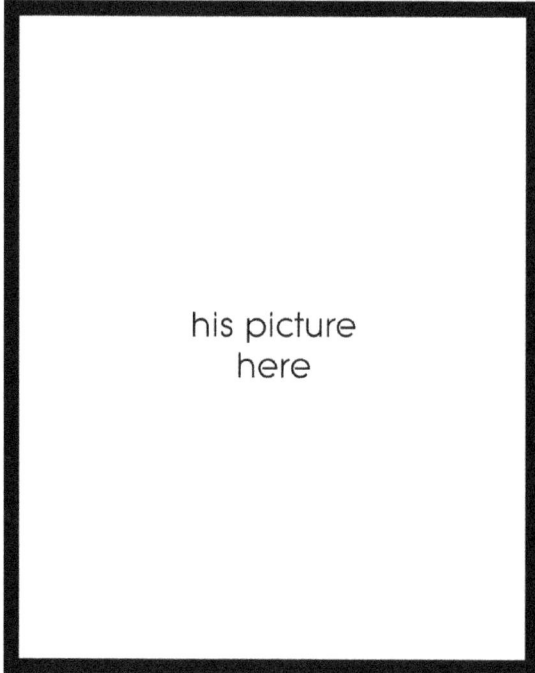

his picture
here

His Name

_____

First   Middle   Last

His Birthdate

_____

Month   Day   Year

He was born in...

_____

City, State, Country

♥ His Brothers/Sisters ♥

⧉ His Cousins ⧉

About Great-Great Grandma

My Mom's Great Grandma

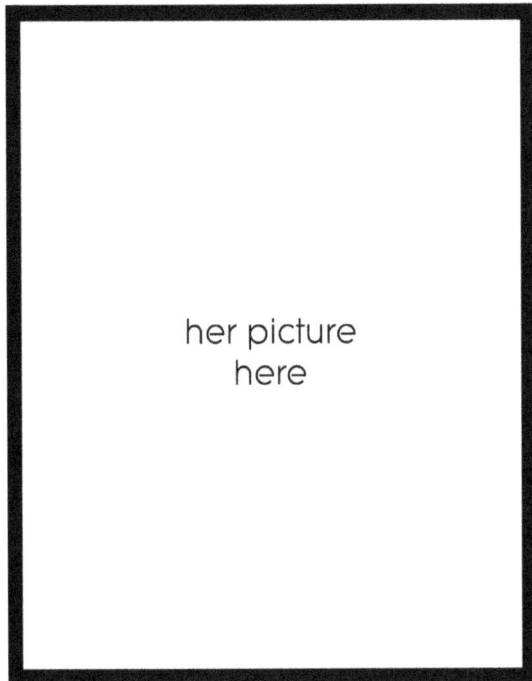

her picture
here

Her Name

_____

First   Middle   Last (Maiden)

Her Birthdate

_____

Month   Day   Year

She was born in...

_____

City, State, Country

♥ Her Brothers/Sisters ♥

🧩 Her Cousins 🧩

Pookie's Family Tree

mom

Dad

Pookie
_____
Me

My Brother

great grandma

great grandpa

great grandma

grandma

grandpa

great grandpa

dad

me

great grandpa

great grandma

grandma

great grandma

grandpa

mom

great grandpa

More About Me

What year is it right now: _____

My Favorite Color

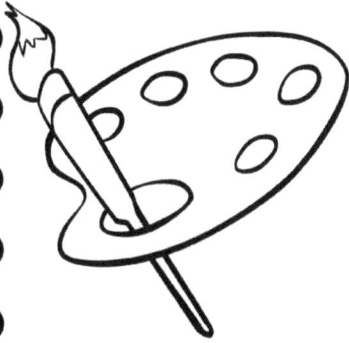

My Favorite Song

My Favorite Movie

January
S M T W T F S

My Favorite Holiday

More About Dad

What year is it right now: _____

His Favorite Color

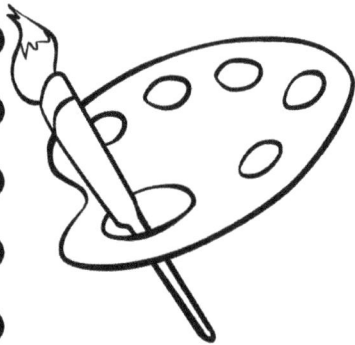

His Favorite Song

His Favorite Movie

His Favorite Holiday

More About Mom

What year is it right now: _____

Her Favorite Color

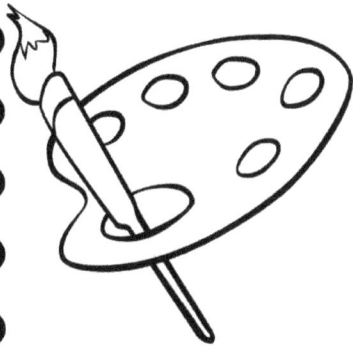

Her Favorite Song

Her Favorite Movie

Her Favorite Holiday

January
S M T W T F S

Memories

Write down, draw, or paste pictures of your memories with your family members

Memories

Memories

 # Memories

 # Memories

 # Memories

 # Memories

Extra Notes

Use these pages to write anything you have discovered about your family.

(Example: My grandpa came over from china when he was 16 years old.)

Extra Notes

Extra Notes

Extra Notes

Extra Notes

Extra Notes

Extra Notes

www.ingramcontent.com/pod-product-compliance
Lightning Source LLC
Chambersburg PA
CBHW040302100426
42811CB00011B/1342